Poems to Share

Poems to Share

Selected by
Susan Dickinson

Illustrated by
Patrice Aggs

Dutton

DUTTON
Published by the Penguin Group
Penguin Books Ltd, 27 Wrights Lane, London w8 5TZ, England
Penguin Books USA Inc., 375 Hudson Street, New York, New York 10014, USA
Penguin Books Australia Ltd, Ringwood, Victoria, Australia
Penguin Books Canada Ltd, 10 Alcorn Avenue, Toronto, Ontario, Canada M4V 3B2
Penguin Books (NZ) Ltd, 182–190 Wairau Road, Auckland 10, New Zealand

First published 1995
1 3 5 7 9 10 8 6 4 2

This collection copyright © Susan Dickinson, 1995
Illustrations copyright © Patrice Aggs, 1995

The Acknowledgements on pp. 111–112 constitute an extension of this copyright page

All rights reserved.
Without limiting the rights under copyright
reserved above, no part of this publication may be
reproduced, stored in or introduced into a retrieval system,
or transmitted, in any form or by any means (electronic, mechanical,
photocopying, recording or otherwise), without the prior
written permission of both the copyright owner
and the above publisher of this book

Filmset by Datix International Limited, Bungay, Suffolk
Printed in England by Clays Ltd, St Ives plc
Set in 14/16 pt Monophoto Plantin

A CIP catalogue record for this book is available from the British Library

ISBN 0–525–69036–0

*C*ontents

*C*reatures   10

Cat	ELEANOR FARJEON	10
Ducks' Ditty	KENNETH GRAHAME	12
Twinkle Twinkle Firefly	JOHN AGARD	13
The Vulture	HILAIRE BELLOC	14
Suzie's New Dog	JOHN CIARDI	15
The Donkey	ANONYMOUS	16
What Became of Them?	ANONYMOUS	17
Rats!	ROBERT BROWNING	18
Five Eyes	WALTER DE LA MARE	19
The Cow	ROBERT LOUIS STEVENSON	20
Snorri Pig	ANONYMOUS	21
The Owl	ALFRED, LORD TENNYSON	22
Crab	TED HUGHES	23
The Caterpillar	CHRISTINA ROSSETTI	24
A Centipede	ANONYMOUS	25

*M*oonshine and Magic   26

The Witches' Ride	KARLA KUSKIN	26
Double, Double Toil and Trouble	WILLIAM SHAKESPEARE	27
Overheard on a Saltmarsh	HAROLD MONRO	28
The Ride-By-Nights	WALTER DE LA MARE	29
The Stone Troll	J. R. R. TOLKIEN	30
Beltane Eve	W. CROFT DICKINSON	32
Ariel's Song	WILLIAM SHAKESPEARE	33

Out of Doors — 34

Seeds	Walter de la Mare	34
A Boy's Song	James Hogg	35
Loveliest of Trees	A. E. Housman	36
Cat and Crocuses	Eva Martin	37
A Green Cornfield	Christina Rossetti	38
Cuckoo Song	Anonymous	39
Adlestrop	Edward Thomas	40
A Hot Day	A. S. J. Tessimond	41
The Rain	W. H. Davies	42
Mud	Polly Chase Boyden	43
Wind	Ted Hughes	44
Windy Nights	Robert Louis Stevenson	46
Storm	Roger McGough	47
Ancient Music	Ezra Pound	48
Winter Morning	Ogden Nash	49
Working in Winter	John Mole	49

Stuff and Nonsense — 50

Jim Jay	Walter de la Mare	50
The Duel	Eugene Field	52
The Lobster Quadrille	Lewis Carroll	54
The Table and the Chair	Edward Lear	56
The Cat and the Pig	Gerard Benson	58
The Swapping Song	Kentucky Mountain Song	60
Henry King	Hilaire Belloc	62
The Poultries	Ogden Nash	63

Sing a Song of People — 64

Sing a Song of People	LOIS LENSKI	64
Clumsy Clarissa	COLIN WEST	66
On Jessy Watson's Elopement	MARJORY FLEMING	67
Little Willie	ANONYMOUS	67
Waltzing Matilda	A. B. PATERSON	68
The Skyfoogle	MICHAEL ROSEN	70
The Firemen	JAMES K. BAXTER	72
The Farmer's Boy	OLD SONG	74
Teevee	EVE MERRIAM	76
I Saw a Jolly Hunter	CHARLES CAUSLEY	77

Friends and Family — 78

My Father	TED HUGHES	78
Mothers Who Don't Understand	AUGUSTA SKYE	80
Missing Mama	ELOISE GREENFIELD	82
Poor Grandma	GRACE NICHOLS	83
Granny	SPIKE MILLIGAN	84
Granny	GRACE NICHOLS	85
The Friday Night Smell	MARC MATTHEWS	86
The Fridge	JOHN MOLE	88
The Rival Arrives	BRIAN PATTEN	89
When Boss Away, Jackass Take Holiday	JOHN AGARD	90
The Leader	ROGER MCGOUGH	91
Rope Rhyme	ELOISE GREENFIELD	91

What Jenny Knows	JACKIE KAY	92
When	SHELAGH MCGEE	94
Frank	COLIN WEST	95

Here and There 96

Where Go the Boats?	ROBERT LOUIS STEVENSON	96
The Lake Isle of Innisfree	WILLIAM BUTLER YEATS	97
Stopping by Woods on a Snowy Evening	ROBERT FROST	98
Mouse's Nest	JOHN CLARE	99
Fisherman's Tale	IRENE RAWNSLEY	100
Ducks Don't Shop in Sainsbury's	GARY BOSWELL	101
Vailima	ROBERT LOUIS STEVENSON	102
My Heart's in the Highlands	ROBERT BURNS	103
Moving	JENNIFER CURRY	104
School Trip	PETER DIXON	106

Index of First Lines	108
Acknowledgements	111

Creatures

Cat

Cat!
Scat!
Atter her, atter her,
Sleeky flatterer,
Spitfire chatterer,
Scatter her, scatter her,
    Off her mat!
    Wuff!
    Wuff!
    Treat her rough!
Git her, git her,
Whiskery spitter!
Catch her, catch her,
Green-eyed scratcher!
    Slathery
    Slithery
    Hisser,
    Don't miss her!

Run till you're dithery,
    Hithery
    Thithery
    Pfitts! Pfitts!
    How she spits!
    Spitch! Spatch!
    Can't she scratch!

Scritching the bark
Of the sycamore-tree,
She's reached her ark
And's hissing at me
    Pfitts! Pfitts!
    Wuff! Wuff!
    Scat,
    Cat!
    That's
    That!

    ELEANOR FARJEON

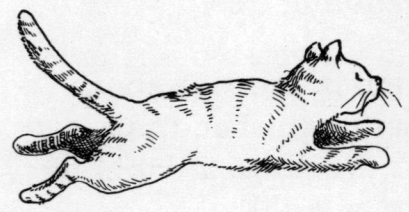

Ducks' Ditty

All along the backwater,
Through the rushes tall,
Ducks are a-dabbling.
Up tails all!

Ducks' tails, drakes' tails,
Yellow feet a-quiver,
Yellow bills all out of sight
Busy in the river!

Slushy green undergrowth
Where the roach swim –
Here we keep our larder,
Cool and full and dim.

Every one for what he likes!
We like to be
Heads down, tails up,
Dabbling free!

High in the blue above
Swifts whirl and call –
We are down a-dabbling
Up tails all!

                Kenneth Grahame

Twinkle Twinkle Firefly

Twinkle
Twinkle
Firefly
In the dark
It's you I spy

Over the river
Over the bush

Twinkle
Twinkle
Firefly
For the traveller
passing by

Over the river
Over the bush

Twinkle
Twinkle
Firefly
Lend the dark
your sparkling eye

    JOHN AGARD

The Vulture

The Vulture eats between his meals,
   And that's the reason why
He very, very rarely feels
   As well as you and I.

His eye is dull, his head is bald,
   His neck is growing thinner.
Oh! What a lesson for us all
   To only eat at dinner!

                HILAIRE BELLOC

Suzie's New Dog

Your dog? What dog? You mean it? – that!
　　I was about to leave a note
Pinned to a fish to warn my cat
　　To watch for a mouse in an overcoat!

So that's a dog! Is it any breed
　　That anyone ever knew – or guessed?
Oh, a Flea Terrier! Yes indeed.
　　Well now, I *am* impressed!

I guess no robber will try your house
　　Or even cut through your yard.
Not when he knows you have a mouse
　　– I mean a dog – like that on guard!

You have to go? I'm glad you came!
　　I don't see a thing like that
Just every day. Does it have a name?
　　Fang, eh? Well, I must warn my cat.

　　　　　　　　　　　　JOHN CIARDI

The Donkey

I saw a donkey
One day old,
His head was too big
For his neck to hold;
His legs were shaky
And long and loose,
They rocked and staggered
And weren't much use.

He tried to gambol
And frisk a bit,
But he wasn't quite sure
Of the trick of it.
His queer little coat
Was soft and grey,
And he curled at his neck
In a lovely way.

He looked so little
And weak and slim,
I prayed the world
Might be good to him.

          ANONYMOUS

What Became of Them?

He was a rat, and she was a rat,
  And down in one hole they did dwell,
And both were as black as a witch's cat,
  And they loved each other well.

He had a tail, and she had a tail,
  Both long and curling and fine;
And each said, 'Yours is the finest tail
  In the world, excepting mine.'

He smelt the cheese, and she smelt the cheese,
  And they both pronounced it good;
And both remarked it would greatly add
  To the charms of their daily food.

So he ventured out, and she ventured out,
  And I saw them go with pain;
But what befell them I never can tell,
  For they never came back again.

                              ANONYMOUS

Rats!

Into the street the Piper stept,
Smiling first a little smile,
As if he knew what magic slept
In his quiet pipe the while;
Then, like a musical adept,
To blow the pipe his lips he wrinkled,
And green and blue his sharp eyes twinkled
Like a candle-flame where salt is sprinkled;
And ere three shrill notes the pipe uttered,
You heard as if an army muttered;
And the muttering grew to a grumbling;
And the grumbling grew to a mighty rumbling;
And out of the houses the rats came tumbling.
Great rats, small rats, lean rats, brawny rats,
Brown rats, black rats, grey rats, tawny rats,
Grave old plodders, gay young friskers,
Fathers, mothers, uncles, cousins,
Cocking tails and pricking whiskers,
Families by tens and dozens,
Brothers, sisters, husbands, wives –
Followed the Piper for their lives.
From street to street he piped advancing,
And step for step they followed dancing,
Until they came to the river Weser
Wherein all plunged and perished!

ROBERT BROWNING
from *The Pied Piper of Hamelin*

Five Eyes

In Hans' old mill his three black cats
Watch his bins for the thieving rats.
Whisker and claw, they crouch in the night,
Their five eyes smouldering green and bright:
Squeaks from the flour sacks, squeaks from where
The cold wind stirs on the empty stair,
Squeaking and scampering, everywhere.
Then down they pounce, now in, now out,
At whisking tail, and sniffing snout;
While lean old Hans he snores away
Till peep of light at break of day;
Then up he climbs to his creaking mill,
Out come his cats all grey with meal –
Jekkel, and Jessup, and one-eyed Jill.

WALTER DE LA MARE

The Cow

The friendly cow, all red and white,
I love with all my heart:
She gives me cream with all her might,
To eat with apple-tart.

She wanders lowing here and there,
And yet she cannot stray,
All in the pleasant open air,
The pleasant light of day;

And blown by all the winds that pass
And wet with all the showers,
She walks among the meadow grass
And eats the meadow flowers.

ROBERT LOUIS STEVENSON

Snorri Pig

Snorri Pig had a curly tail,
   A curly tail, a curly tail,
His head was round as the top of a pail,
   Hey up for Snorri Pig!

Snorri Pig had big brown eyes,
   Big brown eyes, big brown eyes,
And he was jarl of all the sties,
   Hey up for Snorri Pig!

When Snorri Pig met a lady sow,
   A lady sow, a lady sow,
He'd smile and bend his knees full low,
   Hey up for Snorri Pig!

But when he met another boar,
   Another boar, another boar,
He'd tread him into the farmyard floor,
   Hey up for Snorri Pig!

ANONYMOUS

jarl: lord

The Owl

When cats run home and light is come,
  And dew is cold upon the ground,
And the far-off stream is dumb,
  And the whirring sail goes round,
  And the whirring sail goes round:
    Alone and warming his five wits,
    The white owl in the belfry sits.

When merry milkmaids click the latch,
  And rarely smells the new-mown hay,
And the cock hath sung beneath the thatch
  Twice or thrice his roundelay,
  Twice or thrice his roundelay:
    Alone and warming his five wits,
    The white owl in the belfry sits.

ALFRED, LORD TENNYSON

Crab

In the low tide pools
I pack myself like
A handy pocket
Chest of tools.

But as the tide fills
Dancing I go
Under lifted veils
Tiptoe, tiptoe.

And with pliers and pincers
Repair and remake
The daintier dancers
The breakers break.

                    TED HUGHES

The Caterpillar

Brown and furry
Caterpillar, in a hurry
Take your walk
To the shady leaf or stalk
Or what not,
Which may be the chosen spot.
No toad spy you,
Hovering bird of prey pass by you;
Spin and die,
To live again a butterfly.

CHRISTINA ROSSETTI

A Centipede

A centipede was happy quite,
    Until a frog in fun
Said, 'Pray, which leg comes after which?'
This raised her mind to such a pitch,
She lay distracted in the ditch
    Considering how to run.

                                    ANONYMOUS

Moonshine and Magic

The Witches' Ride

Over the hills
Where the edge of the light
Deepens and darkens
To ebony night,
Narrow hats high
Above yellow bead eyes,
The tatter-haired witches
Ride through the skies.
Over the seas
Where the flat fishes sleep
Wrapped in the slap of the slippery deep,
Over the peaks
Where the black trees are bare,
Where boney birds quiver
They glide through the air.
Silently humming
A horrible tune,
They sweep through the stillness
To sit on the moon.

KARLA KUSKIN

Double, Double Toil and Trouble

Double, double toil and trouble;
Fire burn and cauldron bubble.

Round about the cauldron go;
In the poisoned entrails throw.
Toad, that under cold stone
Days and nights hast thirty-one
Swelter'd venom sleeping got,
Boil thou first i' the charmed pot.

Double, double toil and trouble;
Fire burn and cauldron bubble.

Fillet of a fenny snake,
In the cauldron boil and bake;
Eye of newt, and toe of frog,
Wool of bat, and tongue of dog,
Adder's fork, and blind-worm's sting,
Lizard's leg and howlet's wing,
For a charm of powerful trouble,
Like a hell-broth boil and bubble.

Double, double toil and trouble;
Fire burn and cauldron bubble.

WILLIAM SHAKESPEARE
from *Macbeth*

Overheard on a Saltmarsh

Nymph, nymph, what are your beads?

Green glass, goblin. Why do you stare at them?

Give them me.

      No.

Give them me. Give them me.

           No.

Then I will howl all night in the reeds.
Lie in the mud and howl for them.

Goblin, why do you love them so?

They are better than stars or water,
Better than voices of winds that sing,
Better than any man's fair daughter,
Your green glass beads on a silver ring.

Hush, I stole them out of the moon.

Give me your beads. I desire them.

           No.

I will howl in a deep lagoon
For your green glass beads, I love them so.
Give them me. Give them.

No.

HAROLD MONRO

The Ride-by-Nights

Up on their brooms the Witches stream,
Crooked and black in the crescent's gleam;
One foot high, and one foot low,
Bearded, cloaked, and cowled, they go.
'Neath Charlie's Wain they twitter and tweet,
And away they swarm 'neath the Dragon's feet.
With a whoop and a flutter they swing and sway,
And surge pell-mell down the Milky Way.
Betwixt the legs of the glittering Chair
They hover and squeak in the empty air.
Then round they swoop past the glimmering Lion
To where Sirius barks behind huge Orion;
Up, then, and over to wheel amain,
Under the silver, and home again.

WALTER DE LA MARE

The Stone Troll

Troll sat alone on his seat of stone,
And munched and mumbled a bare old bone;
   For many a year he had gnawed it near,
     For meat was hard to come by.
        Done by! Gum by!
   In a cave in the hills he dwelt alone,
     And meat was hard to come by.

Up came Tom with his big boots on.
Said he to Troll: 'Pray, what is yon?
   For it looks like the shin o' my nuncle Tim,
     As should be a-lyin' in graveyard.
        Caveyard! Paveyard!
   This many a year has Tim been gone,
     And I thought he were lyin' in graveyard.'

'My lad,' said Troll, 'this bone I stole.
But what be bones that lie in a hole?
   Thy nuncle was dead as a lump o' lead,
     Afore I found his shinbone.
        Tinbone! Thinbone!
   He can spare a share for a poor old troll;
     For he don't need his shinbone.'

Said Tom: 'I don't see why the likes o' thee
Without axin' leave should go makin' free
   With the shank or the shin o' my father's kin;
     So hand the old bone over!
        Rover! Trover!
   Though dead he be, it belongs to he;
     So hand the old bone over!'

'For a couple o' pins,' says Troll, and grins,
'I'll eat thee too, and gnaw thy shins.
   A bit o' fresh meat will go down sweet!
     I'll try my teeth on thee now.
        Hee now! See now!
   I'm tired o' gnawing old bones and skins;
     I've a mind to dine on thee now.'

But just as he thought his dinner was caught,
He found his hands had hold of naught.
   Before he could mind, Tom slipped behind
     And gave him the boot to larn him.
        Warn him! Darn him!
   A bump o' the boot on the seat, Tom thought,
     Would be the way to larn him.

But harder than stone is the flesh and bone
Of a troll that sits in the hills alone.
   As well set your boot to the mountain's root,
     For the seat of a troll don't feel it.
        Peel it! Heal it!
   Old Troll laughed, when he heard Tom groan,
     And he knew his toes could feel it.

Tom's leg is game, since home he came,
And his bootless foot is lasting lame;
   But Troll don't care, and he's still there
     With the bone he boned from its owner.
        Doner! Boner!
   Troll's old seat is still the same,
     And the bone he boned from its owner!

                    J. R. R. TOLKIEN

Beltane Eve

Dig the ditch and raise the mound;
Form the ring in elfin ground.
Light the fires of burning brands
Where the Nine-Stone-Circle stands.

Who dare pass the fires between?
Who dare reach the magic green?
Who dare dance on magic ground
In the Nine-Stone-Circle round?

On Beltane Eve when eagles fly
On awful errands through the sky,
The White King's host will win the fight
And put the Black King's horde to flight.

Black is death, cold Winter's black;
White is life, warm Summer's white.
The Beltane trees with burning light
Bid Winter flee, call Summer back.

Who will pass the fires between?
Who will dance on magic green?
He shall see the long ago
Beyond the Circle's Beltane glow.

W. Croft Dickinson

Beltane is a Celtic festival held at the beginning of May when the White King of Summer must defeat the Black King of Winter.

Ariel's Song

Where the bee sucks, there suck I:
In a cowslip's bell I lie;
There I couch when owls do cry.
On the bat's back I do fly
After summer merrily:
Merrily, merrily shall I live now
Under the blossom that hangs on the bough.

WILLIAM SHAKESPEARE
from *The Tempest*

Out of Doors

Seeds

The seeds I sowed –
For weeks unseen –
Have pushed up pygmy
Shoots of green:
So frail you'd think
The tiniest stone
Would never let
A glimpse be shown.
But no; a pebble
Near them lies,
At least a cherry-stone
In size,
Which that mere sprout
Has heaved away,
To bask in sunshine,
See the Day.

WALTER DE LA MARE

A Boy's Song

Where the pools are bright and deep,
Where the grey trout lies asleep,
Up the river and over the lea,
That's the way for Billy and me.

Where the blackbird sings the latest,
Where the hawthorn blooms the sweetest,
Where the nestlings chirp and flee,
That's the way for Billy and me.

Where the mowers mow the cleanest,
Where the hay lies thick and greenest;
There to trace the homeward bee,
That's the way for Billy and me.

Where the hazel bank is steepest,
Where the shadow falls the deepest,
Where the clustering nuts fall free,
That's the way for Billy and me.

Why the boys should drive away
Little sweet maidens from the play,
Or love to banter and fight so well,
That's the thing I never could tell.

But this I know, I love to play,
Through the meadow, among the hay:
Up the water and over the lea,
That's the way for Billy and me.

JAMES HOGG

Loveliest of Trees

Loveliest of trees, the cherry now
Is hung with bloom along the bough,
And stands about the woodland ride
Wearing white for Eastertide.

Now, of my threescore years and ten,
Twenty will not come again,
And take from seventy springs a score,
It only leaves me fifty more.

And since to look at things in bloom
Fifty springs are little room,
About the woodlands I will go
To see the cherry hung with snow.

     A. E. Housman
     from *A Shropshire Lad*

Cat and Crocuses

In the crocus-bed I saw her:
Like a queen enthroned she sat.
Yellow crocuses shone round her –
Royal, sun-illumined cat:

Orange eyes intensely lighted
By a vivid golden flame:
Fire of spring that burnt within her,
And in every flower the same.

World-surveying, world contented,
Seated in her crocus ring:
Cat and crocuses together
Basking in the fires of spring.

EVA MARTIN

A Green Cornfield

The earth was green, the sky was blue:
   I saw and heard one sunny morn
A skylark hang between the two,
   A singing speck above the corn.

A stage below, in gay accord,
   White butterflies danced on the wing,
And still the singing skylark soared,
   And silent sank and soared to sing.

The cornfield stretched a tender green
   To right and left beside my walks;
I knew he had a nest unseen
   Somewhere among the million stalks.

And as I paused to hear his song
   While swift the sunny moments slid,
Perhaps his mate sat listening long,
   And listened longer than I did.

CHRISTINA ROSSETTI

Cuckoo Song

Summer is icumen in,
Lhude sing cuccu!
Groweth sede and bloweth mede,
And springeth wood anu –
    Sing: cuccu!

Ewe bleteth after lamb,
Loweth after calve cu;
Bullock sterteth, bucke verteth,
Merrie sing cuccu!

Cuccu, cuccu, well singes thou, cuccu;
Ne swike thou never nu;
Sing cuccu, nu, sing cuccu,
Sing cuccu, sing cuccu, nu!

                    ANONYMOUS

cu: cow
sterteth: jumps
verteth: leaps
swike: stop
nu: now

This poem was written in the thirteenth century. It is one of the first poems to have been written in English. Compare it with 'Ancient Music' on page 48.

Adlestrop

Yes. I remember Adlestrop —
The name, because one afternoon
Of heat the express-train drew up there
Unwontedly. It was late June.

The steam hissed. Someone cleared his throat.
No one left and no one came
On the bare platform. What I saw
Was Adlestrop — only the name

And willows, willow-herb, and grass,
And meadowsweet, and haycocks dry,
No whit less still and lonely fair
Than the high cloudlets in the sky.

And for that minute a blackbird sang
Close by, and round him, mistier,
Farther and farther, all the birds
Of Oxfordshire and Gloucestershire.

EDWARD THOMAS

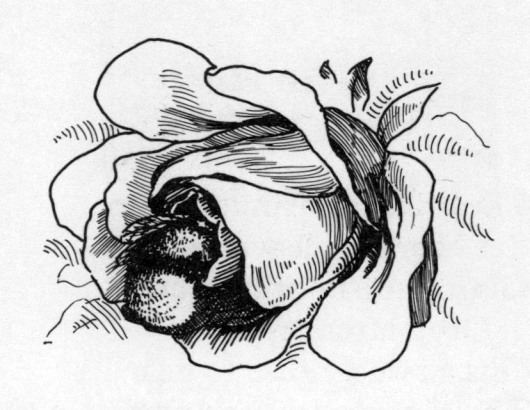

A Hot Day

Cottonwool clouds loiter.
A lawnmower, very far,
Birrs. Then a bee comes
To a crimson rose and softly
Deftly and fatly crams
A velvet body in.

A tree, June-lazy, makes
A tent of dim green light.
Sunlight weaves in the leaves,
Honey-light laced with leaf-light,
Green interleaved with gold.
Sunlight gathers its rays
In sheaves, which the wind unweaves
And then reweaves – the wind
That puffs a smell of grass
Through the heat-heavy, trembling
Summer pool of air.

A. S. J. Tessimond

The Rain

I hear leaves drinking rain;
   I hear rich leaves on top
Giving the poor beneath
   Drop after drop;
'Tis a sweet noise to hear
These green leaves drinking near.

And when the Sun comes out,
   After this rain shall stop,
A wondrous light will fill
   Each dark, round drop;
I hope the Sun shines bright;
'Twill be a lovely sight.

                W. H. DAVIES

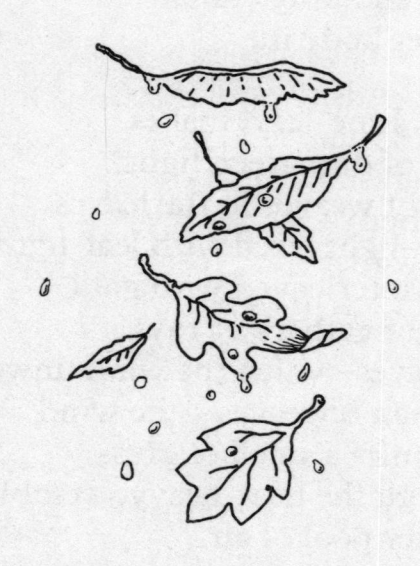

Mud

Mud is very nice to feel
All squishy-squash between the toes!
I'd rather wade in wiggly mud
Than smell a yellow rose.
Nobody else but the rosebush knows
How nice mud feels
Between the toes.

POLLY CHASE BOYDEN

Wind

This house has been far out at sea all night,
The woods crashing through darkness, the
   booming hills,
Winds stampeding the fields under the window
Floundering black astride and blinding wet

Till day rose; then under an orange sky
The hills had new places, and wind wielded
Blade-like, luminous black and emerald,
Flexing like the lens of a mad eye.

At noon I scaled along the house-side as far as
The coal-house door. I dared once to look up –
Through the brunt wind that dented the balls of
   my eyes
The tent of the hills drummed and strained its
   guyrope,

The fields quivering, the skyline a grimace,
At any second to bang and vanish with a flap:
The wind flung a magpie away and a black-
Back gull bent like an iron bar slowly. The house

Rang like some fine green goblet in the note
That any second would shatter it. Now deep
In chairs, in front of the great fire, we grip
Our hearts and cannot entertain book, thought,

Or each other. We watch the fire blazing,
And feel the roots of the house move, but sit on,
Seeing the window tremble to come in,
Hearing the stones cry out under the horizons.

       TED HUGHES

Windy Nights

Whenever the moon and stars are set,
  Whenever the wind is high,
All night long in the dark and wet,
  A man goes riding by.
Late in the night when the fires are out,
  Why does he gallop and gallop about?

Whenever the trees are crying aloud,
  And ships are tossed at sea,
By, on the highway, low and loud,
  By at the gallop goes he.
By at the gallop he goes, and then
By he comes back at the gallop again.

ROBERT LOUIS STEVENSON

Storm

They're at it again
the wind and the rain
It all started
when the wind
took the window
by the collar
and shook it
with all its might
Then the rain
butted in
What a din
they'll be at it all night
Serves them right
if they go home in the morning
and the sky won't let them in

ROGER MCGOUGH

Ancient Music

After a medieval song

Winter is icumen in,
Lhude sing Goddamm,
Raineth drop and staineth slop,
And how the wind doth ramm!
          Sing: Goddamm.

Skiddeth bus and sloppeth us,
An ague hath my ham.
Freezeth river, turneth liver,
          Damn you, sing: Goddamm.

Goddamm, Goddamm, 'tis why I am, Goddamm,
          So against the winter's balm.
Sing goddamm, damm, sing Goddamm,
Sing goddamm, sing goddamm, DAMN.

                                    EZRA POUND

Winter Morning

Winter is the king of showmen,
Turning tree stumps into snow men
And houses into birthday cakes
And spreading sugar over lakes.
Smooth and clean and frosty white,
The world looks good enough to bite.
That's the season to be young,
Catching snowflakes on your tongue.
Snow is snowy when it's snowing
I'm sorry it's slushy when it's going.

                OGDEN NASH

Working in Winter

Silently the snow settles on the scaffolding,
The feathery flakes flurry and flick their
   fragments,
The brown bricks piled on billowing polythene
Heap their heaviness to heavenly heights.
Workmen in woolly hats whistle into the wind
Or dance in donkey jackets to hold in heat,
Their toes tingle, the tips of their fingers freeze –
It's murder, mate, this job is, murder.
Roll on five o'clock!

                JOHN MOLE

Stuff and Nonsense

Jim Jay

Do diddle di do,
   Poor Jim Jay
Got stuck fast
   In Yesterday.
Squinting he was,
   On cross-legs bent,
Never heeding
   The wind was spent.
Round veered the weathercock,
   The sun drew in –
And stuck was Jim
   Like a rusty pin . . .
We pulled and we pulled
   From seven till twelve,

Jim, too frightened
   To help himself.
But all in vain.
   The clock struck one,
And there was Jim
   A little bit gone.
At half-past five
   You scarce could see
A glimpse of his flapping
   Handkerchee.
And when came noon,
   And we climbed sky-high,
Jim was a speck
   Slip-slipping by.
Come tomorrow,
   The neighbours say,
He'll be past crying for;
   Poor Jim Jay.

       WALTER DE LA MARE

The Duel

The gingham dog and the calico cat
    Side by side on the table sat;
  'Twas half-past twelve, and (what do you
      think!)
Nor one nor t'other had slept a wink!
    The old Dutch clock and the Chinese plate
    Appeared to know as sure as fate
There was going to be a terrible spat.
    (*I wasn't there; I simply state
    What was told to me by the Chinese plate!*)

The gingham dog went 'bow-wow-wow!'
And the calico cat replied 'mee-ow!'
The air was littered, an hour or so,
With bits of gingham and calico,
    While the old Dutch clock in the chimney-place
    Up with its hands before its face,
For it always dreaded a family row!
    (*Now mind: I'm only telling you
    What the old Dutch clock declares is true!*)

The Chinese plate looked very blue,
And wailed, 'Oh dear! what shall we do!'
But the gingham dog and the calico cat
Wallowed this way and tumbled that,
Employing every tooth and claw
In the awfullest way you ever saw –
And, oh! how the gingham and calico flew!
   (*Don't fancy I exaggerate –*
   I got my news from the Chinese plate!)

Next morning, where the two had sat
They found no trace of dog or cat;
And some folks think unto this day
That burglars stole that pair away!
   But the truth about the cat and pup
   Is this: they ate each other up!
Now what do you really think of that!
   (*The old Dutch clock it told me so,*
   And that is how I came to know.)

EUGENE FIELD

The Lobster Quadrille

'Will you walk a little faster?' said a whiting to a snail.
'There's a porpoise close behind us, and he's treading on my tail.
See how eagerly the lobsters and the turtles all advance!
They are waiting on the shingle – will you come and join the dance?
   Will you, won't you, will you, won't you, will you join the dance?
   Will you, won't you, will you, won't you, won't you join the dance?

'You can really have no notion how delightful it will be,
When they take us up and throw us, with the lobsters, out to sea!'
But the snail replied 'Too far, too far!' and gave a look askance –
Said he thanked the whiting kindly, but he would not join the dance.
   Would not, could not, would not, could not, would not join the dance.
   Would not, could not, would not, could not, could not join the dance.

'What matters it how far we go?' his scaly friend
    replied.
'There is another shore, you know, upon the other
    side.
The further off from England the nearer is to
    France –
Then turn not pale, beloved snail, but come and
    join the dance.
    Will you, won't you, will you, won't you, will
        you join the dance?
    Will you, won't you, will you, won't you, won't
        you join the dance?'

LEWIS CARROLL

The Table and the Chair

I

Said the Table to the Chair,
'You can hardly be aware,
'How I suffer from the heat,
'And from chilblains on my feet!
'If we took a little walk,
'We might have a little talk!
'Pray let us take the air!'
Said the Table to the Chair.

II

Said the Chair unto the Table,
'Now you *know* we are not able!
'How foolishly you talk,
'When you know we *cannot* walk!'
Said the Table, with a sigh,
'It can do no harm to try,
'I've as many legs as you,
'Why can't we walk on two?'

III

So they both went slowly down,
And walked about the town
With a cheerful bumpy sound,
As they toddled round and round.
And everybody cried,
As they hastened to their side,
'See! the Table and the Chair
'Have come out to take the air!'

IV
But in going down an alley,
To a castle in a valley,
They completely lost their way,
And wandered all the day,
Till, to see them safely back,
They paid a Ducky-quack,
And a Beetle, and a Mouse,
Who took them to their house.

V
Then they whispered to each other,
'O delightful little brother!
'What a lovely walk we've taken!
'Let us dine on Beans and Bacon!'
So the Ducky, and the leetle
Browny-Mousy and the Beetle
Dined, and danced upon their heads
Till they toddled to their beds.

EDWARD LEAR

The Cat and the Pig

Once, when I wasn't very big
I made a song about a pig
    Who ate a fig
    And wore a wig
And nimbly danced the Irish jig.

And when I was as small as THAT
I made a verse about a cat
    Who ate a rat
    And wore a hat
And sat (you've guessed) upon the mat.

    And that, I thought, was that.

But yesterday upon my door
I heard a knock; I looked and saw
    A hatted cat
    A wigged pig
    Who chewed a rat
    Who danced the jig
    On my door mat!

They looked at me with faces wise
Out of their bright inquiring eyes.
'May we come in? For we are yours,
Pray do not leave us out of doors.
We are the children of your mind
Let us come in. Be kind. Be kind.'

So now upon my fireside mat
There lies a tireless pussy cat
Who all day long chews on a rat
    And wears a hat.
And round him like a whirligig
Dancing a frantic Irish jig
Munching a fig, cavorts a big
    Wig-headed pig.

They eat my cakes and drink my tea.
There's hardly anything for me!
And yet I cannot throw them out
For they are mine without a doubt.

But when I'm at my desk tonight
I'll be more careful what I write.

I'll be more careful what I write.

                         GERARD BENSON

The Swapping Song

My father he died, but I never knew how.
He left me six horses to drive in my plough.
   With a wim, wam, waddle-o,
   Stick, stock, straddle-o,
   Fin, fan, faddle-o,
   Over the brow!

I sold my six horses and bought me a cow
To make me a fortune but I didn't know how.
   With a wim, wam, waddle-o,
   Stick, stock, straddle-o,
   Fin, fan, faddle-o,
   Over the brow!

I sold my old cow and bought me a calf,
For I never made bargain, but lost the best half.
   With a wim, wam, waddle-o,
   Stick, stock, straddle-o,
   Fin, fan, faddle-o,
   Over the brow!

I sold my calf and bought me a pig,
It wouldn't grow much and it wasn't very big.
   With a wim, wam, waddle-o,
   Stick, stock, straddle-o,
   Fin, fan, faddle-o,
   Over the brow!

I bartered my pig and bought me a cat;
To sit at the fire and to warm her small back.
   With a wim, wam, waddle-o,
   Stick, stock, straddle-o,
   Fin, fan, faddle-o
   Over the brow!

I sold my small cat and bought me a mouse;
His tail caught fire and he burned down my
   house.
   With a wim, wam, waddle-o,
   Stick, stock, straddle-o,
   Fin, fan, faddle-o,
   Over the brow!

                    KENTUCKY MOUNTAIN SONG

Henry King

The Chief Defect of Henry King
Was chewing little bits of String.
At last he swallowed some which tied
Itself in ugly Knots inside.

Physicians of the Utmost Fame
Were called at once; but when they came
They answered, as they took their Fees,
'There is no Cure for this Disease.

'Henry will very soon be dead.'
His Parents stood about his Bed
Lamenting his Untimely Death,
When Henry, with his Latest Breath,

Cried, 'Oh, my Friends, be warned by me,
That Breakfast, Dinner, Lunch, and Tea,
Are all the Human Frame requires . . .'
With that, the Wretched Child expires.

HILAIRE BELLOC

The Poultries

Let's think of eggs.
They have no legs.
Chickens come from eggs
But they have legs.
The plot thickens;
Eggs come from chickens,
But have no legs under 'em.
What a conundrum!

OGDEN NASH

Sing a Song of People

Sing a Song of People

Sing a song of people
 Walking fast or slow;
People in the city,
 Up and down they go.

People on the sidewalk,
People on the bus;
People passing, passing,
In back and front of us.
People on the subway
Underneath the ground;
People riding taxis
Round and round and round.

People with their hats on,
Going in the doors;
People with umbrellas
When it rains and pours.
People in tall buildings
And in stores below;
Riding elevators
Up and down they go.

People walking singly,
People in a crowd;
People saying nothing,
People talking loud.
People laughing, smiling,
Grumpy people too;
People who just hurry
And never look at you!

Sing a song of people
   Who like to come and go;
Sing of city people
   You see but never know!

                LOIS LENSKI

Clumsy Clarissa

Clarissa did the washing up:
She smashed a plate and chipped a cup,
And dropped a glass and cracked a mug,
Then pulled the handle off a jug.
She couldn't do much worse, you'd think,
But then she went and broke the sink.

COLIN WEST

On Jessy Watson's Elopement

Run of is Jessy Watson fair
Her eyes do sparkel, she's good hair.
But Mrs Leath you shal now be
Now and for all Eternity!

MARJORY FLEMING (age 7)

Marjory Fleming (1803–11) lived in Kirkcaldy, Scotland, and died when she was only eight and three-quarters. She wrote a daily journal and many poems, including one on Mary Queen of Scots.

Little Willie

Little Willie from his mirror
Licked the mercury right off,
Thinking, in his childish error,
It would cure the whooping cough.

At the funeral his mother
Brightly said to Mrs Brown:
' 'Twas a chilly day for Willie
When the mercury went down!'

ANONYMOUS

Waltzing Matilda

Oh! There once was a swagman camped in a
   billabong,
Under the shade of a Coolabah tree;
And he sang as he looked at his old billy boiling,
'Who'll come a-waltzing Matilda with me?'

Who'll come a-waltzing Matilda, my darling,
Who'll come a-waltzing Matilda with me?
Waltzing Matilda and leading a water-bag –
Who'll come a-waltzing Matilda with me?

Down came a jumbuck to drink at the water-hole,
Up jumped the swagman and grabbed him in glee;
And he sang as he stowed him away in his tucker-
   bag,
'You'll come a-waltzing Matilda with me!'

Who'll come a-waltzing Matilda, my darling,
Who'll come a-waltzing Matilda with me?
Waltzing Matilda and leading a water-bag –
Who'll come a-waltzing Matilda with me?

Down came the Squatter a-riding his
   thoroughbred;
Down came Policemen – one, two and three,
'Whose is the jumbuck you've got in your tucker-
   bag?
You'll come a-waltzing Matilda with me.'

Who'll come a-waltzing Matilda, my darling,
Who'll come a-waltzing Matilda with me?
Waltzing Matilda and leading a water-bag –
Who'll come a-waltzing Matilda with me?

But the swagman, he up and jumped in the water-hole,
Drowning himself by the Coolabah tree;
And his ghost may be heard as it sings in the billabong,
'Who'll come a-waltzing Matilda with me?'

A B. PATERSON

swagman: a tramp, or labourer, who carries his belongings in a swag while travelling about looking for work
billabong: a backwater from a river
jumbuck: a sheep
Waltzing Matilda: carrying a swag; Matilda was a type of swag where clothes and personal belongings were wrapped in a long blanket roll and tied at the ends like a Christmas cracker.
squatter: a sheep or cattle farmer

The Skyfoogle

There was a man
who turned up round our way once
put up a tent in the park, he did.
Put up notices all round the streets saying
that he was going to put on show
A TERRIFYING CREATURE!!!!!!
Called:
THE SKYFOOGLE!!!!!!
No one had ever seen this thing before.
The show was on for
two o'clock the next day.

Next day, we all turned up to see
THE FIERCEST ANIMAL IN THE
 WORLD!!!!!!
The man took the money at the door
we all poured into the tent.
There was a kind of stage up one end
with a curtain in front of it.
We all sat down and waited.
The man went off behind the curtain.
Suddenly we all heard a terrible scream.

There was an awful yelling and crying,
there was the noise of chains rattling
and someone shouting.
Suddenly the man came running on to the stage
in front of the curtains.
All his clothes were torn,
there was blood on his face
and he screamed:
Quick, get out
get out
get out of here,
THE SKYFOOGLE HAS ESCAPED!!!!!!

We all got up
and ran out the door
and got away as fast as we could.
By the time we got ourselves together
the man had gone.
We never saw him again.
None of us ever saw our money again either . . .
And none of us have ever seen THE
    SKYFOOGLE!!!!!!

MICHAEL ROSEN

The Firemen

*C*lang! *Clang! Clang!*
Says the red fire bell –
'There's a big fire blazing
At the Grand Hotel!'

The firemen shout
As they tumble out of bed
And slide down the pole
To the fire engine shed.

The fire engine starts
With a cough and a roar
And they all climb aboard
As it shoots from the door.

The firemen's helmets,
The ladders and hoses,
Are brassy and bright
As a jug full of roses.

Whee! Whee! Whee! –
You can hear the cry
Of the siren shrieking
As they hurtle by.

At the Grand Hotel
There is smoke and steam.
Flames at the windows
And people who scream.

The biggest fireman
Carries down
A fat old lady
In her dressing gown.

When the fire is finished
The firemen go
Back through the same streets
Driving slow.

Home at the station
The firemen stay
And polish up the nozzles
For the next fire day.

                JAMES K. BAXTER

The Farmer's Boy

The sun went down beyond yon hill, across yon dreary moor;
Weary and lame a boy there came up to the farmer's door;
'Can you tell me if any there be, that will give me employ,
For to plough and sow, for to reap and mow, and be a farmer's boy?

'My father's dead and mother's left with her five children small;
And what is worse for my mother still, I'm the oldest of them all;
Though little I am, I fear no work, if you'll give me employ,
For to plough and sow, for to reap and mow, and be a farmer's boy.

'And if that you won't me employ, one favour I've to ask,
Will you shelter me till the break of day from this cold winter's blast?
At the break of day I'll trudge away, elsewhere to seek employ,
For to plough and sow, for to reap and mow, and be a farmer's boy.'

The farmer said, 'I'll try the lad, no further let
   him seek,'
'Oh, yes! dear father,' the daughter said, while
   tears ran down her cheek;
'For them that will work it's hard to want, and
   wander for employ,
For to plough and sow, for to reap and mow, and
   be a farmer's boy.'

At length the boy became a man, the good old
   farmer died;
He left the lad the farm he had, and his daughter
   to be his bride;
And now the lad a farmer is, and he smiles and
   thinks with joy,
Of the lucky, lucky day, when he came that way,
   to be a farmer's boy.

OLD SONG

Teevee

In the house
of Mr and Mrs Spouse
he and she
would watch teevee
and never a word
between them spoken
until the day
the set was broken.

Then 'How do you do?'
said he to she,
'I don't believe
that we've met yet.
Spouse is my name.
What's yours?' he asked.

'Why, mine's the same!'
said she to he,
'Do you suppose that we could be – ?'

But the set came suddenly right about,
And so they never did find out.

EVE MERRIAM

I *Saw a Jolly* Hunter

I saw a jolly hunter
With a jolly gun
Walking in the country
In the jolly sun.

In the jolly meadow
Sat a jolly hare.
Saw the jolly hunter.
Took jolly care.

Hunter jolly eager –
Sight of jolly prey.
Forgot gun pointing
Wrong jolly way.

Jolly hunter jolly head
Over heels gone.
Jolly old safety-catch
Not jolly on.

Bang went the jolly gun.
Hunter jolly dead.
Jolly hare got clean away.
Jolly good, I said.

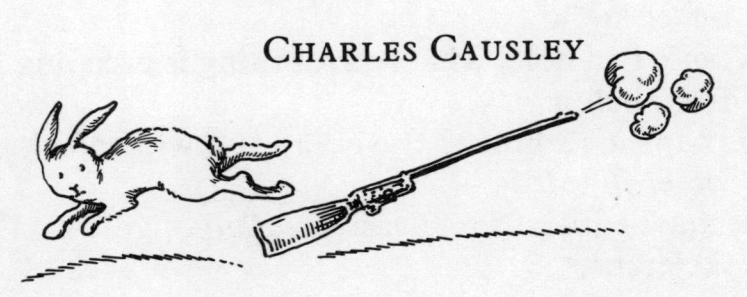

CHARLES CAUSLEY

Friends and Family

My Father

Some fathers work at the office, others work at
  the store,
Some operate great cranes and build up
  skyscrapers galore,
Some work in canning factories counting green
  peas into cans,
Some drive all night in huge and thundering
  removal vans.

But mine has the strangest job of the lot.
My Father's the Chief Inspector of – What?
O don't tell the mice, don't tell the moles,
My Father's the Chief Inspector of HOLES.

It's a work of the highest importance because you
  never know
What's in a hole, what fearful thing is creeping
  from below.
Perhaps it's a hole to the ocean and will soon gush
  water in tons,
Or maybe it leads to a vast cave full of gold and
  skeletons.

    Though a hole might seem to have nothing but dirt in,
Somebody's simply got to make certain.
Caves in the mountain, clefts in the wall,
My Father has to inspect them all.

That crack in the road looks harmless. My Father knows it's not.
The world may be breaking into two and starting at that spot.
Or maybe the world is a great egg, and we live on the shell,
And it's just beginning to split and hatch: you simply cannot tell.

    If you see a crack, run to the phone, run!
My Father will know just what's to be done.
A rumbling hole, a silent hole,
My Father will soon have it under control.

Keeping a check on all these holes he hurries from morning to night.
There might be sounds of marching in one, or an eye shining bright.
A tentacle came groping from a hole that belonged to a mouse,
A floor collapsed and Chinamen swarmed up into the house.

    A Hole's an unpredictable thing –
Nobody knows what a Hole might bring.
Caves in the mountain, clefts in the wall,
My Father has to inspect them all!

                                 TED HUGHES

Mothers Who Don't Understand

'Why can't you tidy your room?' they cry,
Millions of mothers who fret round the land,
'It's a horrible mess, I've never seen worse,'
– Mothers who don't understand.

They don't understand how cosy it is
To have piles of books on the floor,
And knickers and socks making friends with the
   vest
Under the bed, where *they* like it best,
And notices pinned to the door.

They don't understand why Kylie and Craig
Are smiling all over the walls,
And toffees and Chewys and dozens of Smarties
Are scattered about reminding of parties,
And jeans are rolled into balls.

They don't understand why a good bed should be
All scrumpled and friendly and gritty,
Why the bears and the paints and the toys are
   much less
Easy to find if there isn't a mess –
To tidy would be a great pity.

They don't understand the point of a desk
Is to balance the muddle quite high:
To leave the drawers open, grow mould on the
   drink,
Is very much easier, some people think,
Than explaining to mothers just why.

'PLEASE can you tidy your room?' they wail,
Millions of mothers who fret round the land:
'What will you do when there's no one to nag
   you?'
– Mothers who don't understand.

                            AUGUSTA SKYE

Missing Mama

last year when Mama died
I went to my room to hide
from the hurt
I closed my door
wasn't going to come out
no more, never
but my uncle he said
you going to get past
this pain
    you going to
push on past this pain
and one of these days
you going to feel like
yourself again

I don't miss a day
remembering Mama
sometimes I cry
but mostly
I think about
the good things
now

ELOISE GREENFIELD

Poor Grandma

Why this child
so spin-spin spin-spin
Why this child can't keep still

Why this child
so turn-round
turn-round
Why this child
can't settle down

Why this child
can't eat without getting
up to look through window
Why this child must behave so
I want to know
Why this child
so spin-spin spin-spin
Why this child
can't keep still

GRACE NICHOLS

Granny

Through every nook and every cranny
The wind blew in on poor old Granny,
Around her knees, into each ear
(And up her nose as well, I fear).

All through the night the wind grew worse,
It nearly made the vicar curse.
The top had fallen off the steeple
Just missing him (and other people).

It blew on man; it blew on beast.
It blew on nun; it blew on priest.
It blew the wig off Auntie Fanny –
But most of all, it blew on Granny.

SPIKE MILLIGAN

Granny

It so nice to have a Granny
when you've had it from yuh Mammy
and you feeling down and dammy

It so nice to have a Granny
when she brings you bread and jammy
and says, 'Tell it all to Granny.'

GRACE NICHOLS

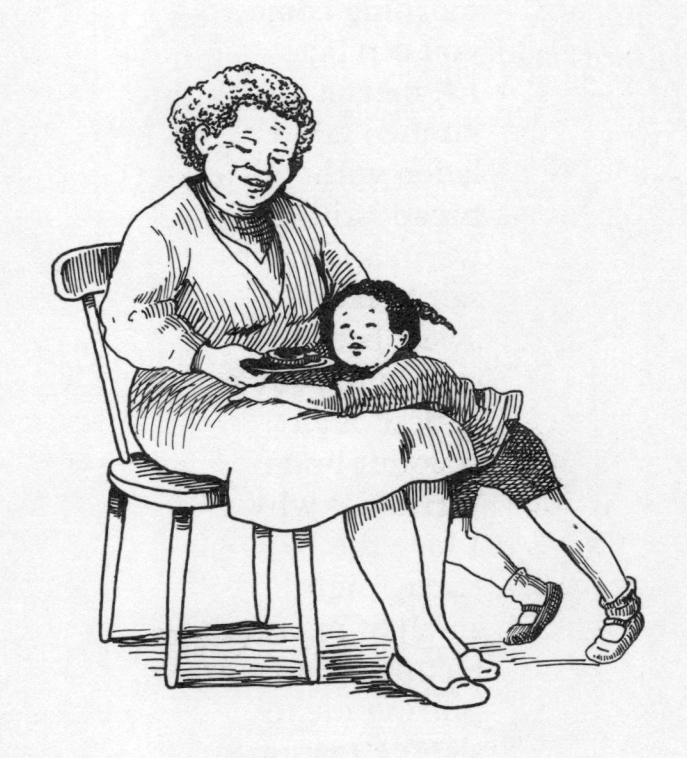

The Friday Night Smell

I love the
friday night
smell of
mammie baking
bread – creeping
up to me in
bed, and tho
zzzz I'll fall
asleep, before I
even get a
bite – when
morning come,
you can bet
I'll meet a
kitchen table
laden with
bread, still
warm and fresh
salt bread
sweet bread
crisp and brown
& best of all
coconut buns
THAT's why
I love the
friday night
smell of mammie
baking bread
putting me to
sleep, dreaming
of jumping from

the highest branch
of the jamoon tree
into the red water
creek
beating carlton
run & catching
the biggest fish
in the world
plus, getting
the answers right
to every single
sum
that every day
in my dream
begins and ends
with the friday
night smell of
mammie baking
bread, and
coconut buns
of course.

MARC MATTHEWS

The Fridge

Into the kitchen
At half-past three
And straight to the fridge –
What's in it for me?

A strawberry yoghurt?
A sticky Swiss Bun?
Oh an Angel Delight
Is my generous Mum!

So I open the door
But a breath of cold air
Is all that I find –
There's nothing there.

Now this really is not
How things should be
When you get home from school
At half-past three.

JOHN MOLE

The Rival Arrives

Tom, take the baby out of the fridge
And put the milk back in.
We know you are not used to him
And think he makes a din,
But I'm afraid he's here to stay
And he is rather cute,
So you'll have to stop insisting
He goes in the car-boot.
And please stop telling all your friends
We bought him in a sale,
Or that he's a free sample
We received in the mail.
He was *not* found in a trolley
At the local Mothercare,
And a family did not give him us
Because they'd one to spare.

You should look on the bright side, Tom.
In just a year or two
You will have someone else to blame
For the wicked things you do.

BRIAN PATTEN

When Boss Away, Jackass Take Holiday

Yay
Teacher gone out the room
now it's monkey bout time
Quick blow up the balloon!

When the cat's away
the mice will play
that's what Teacher would say.

But me Granny does say,
'When the farmer away,
Jackass take holiday.'

A Jackass is a donkey you know
so when the farmer away
donkey won't have to pull
big heavy dray.

Donkey can eat belly full
Donkey ears can glow
Donkey can even dance disco.

JOHN AGARD

The Leader

I wanna be the leader
I wanna be the leader
Can I be the leader?
Can I? Can I?
Promise? Promise?
Yippee, I'm the leader
I'm the leader.

OK what shall we do?

ROGER MCGOUGH

Rope Rhyme

Get set, ready now, jump right in
Bounce and kick and giggle and spin
Listen to the rope when it hits the ground
Listen to that clappedy-slappedy sound
Jump right up when it tells you to
Come back down whatever you do
Count to a hundred, count by ten
Start to count all over again
That's what jumping is all about
Get set, ready now,
                    jump
                          right
                              out!

ELOISE GREENFIELD

What Jenny Knows

'**I** didn't come out my mummy's tummy.
No I didn't,' I says to my pal Jenny.
But Jenny says, 'You must have.
How come?' And I replies,

'I just didn't. Get it. I didn't.'
'Everybody does,' says Jenny,
who is fastly becoming an enemy.
'Rubbish,' I say. 'My mummy got me.

She picked me. She collected me.
I was in a supermarket,
on the shelf and she took me off it.'
'Nonsense,' says Jenny. 'Lies.'

'Are you calling me a liar?'
I'm getting angry. It's not funny.
'No, but you have a tendency'
(a word from her aunty, probably)

'To make things up.'
'Look. I'm speaking the Truth.'
I say, 'Cross my heart.'
'Don't hope to die,' shouts Jenny.

Awful superstitious, so she is.
'I'm adopted,' I says, 'adopted.'
'I know That!' says Jenny.
'But you still came out

Somebody's tummy. Somebody
had to have you. Didn't they?'
'Not my mummy. Not my mummy,' I says.
'Shut your face. Shut your face.'

       JACKIE KAY

When

When I'm an aunt I shan't
Sip tea and criticize,
Won't buy my nieces socks,
Or my nephews ties.
For birthdays I'll send monkeys,
White mice and pirate suits;
At Christmas sets for chemistry,
And tambourines and flutes.
At Easter I'll bring chocolate eggs,
Not hymn books of white leather,
And I'll never scold at muddy feet
Or dogs in rainy weather.
When I'm an aunt I'll never mind
Rough ball games on my lawn,
And even turn an eye that's blind
To pillow fights at dawn.

SHELAGH McGEE

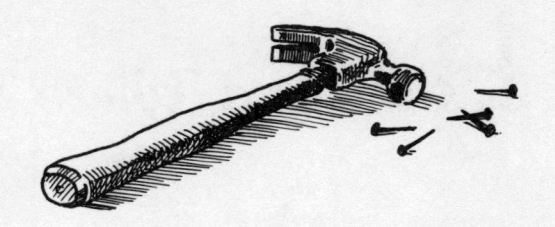

Frank

We don't mention Frank
In this house any more;
No, not since he nailed
Mother's boots to the floor.
What makes matters worse
With regard to this crime
Is Mother was wearing
Her boots at the time.

                Colin West

Here and There

Where Go the Boats?

Dark brown is the river,
  Golden is the sand.
It flows along for ever,
  With trees on either hand.

Green leaves a-floating,
  Castles of the foam,
Boats of mine a-boating –
  Where will all come home?

On goes the river
  And out past the mill,
Away down the valley,
  Away down the hill.

Away down the river,
  A hundred miles or more,
Other little children
  Shall bring my boats ashore.

ROBERT LOUIS STEVENSON

The Lake Isle of Innisfree

I will arise and go now, and go to Innisfree,
And a small cabin build there, of clay and wattles made:
Nine bean-rows will I have there, a hive for the honey-bee,
And live alone in the bee-loud glade.

And I shall have some peace there, for peace comes dropping slow,
Dropping from the veils of the morning to where the cricket sings;
There midnight's all a glimmer, and noon a purple glow,
And evening full of the linnet's wings.

I will arise and go now, for always night and day
I hear lake water lapping with low sounds by the shore;
While I stand on the roadway, or on the pavements grey,
I hear it in the deep heart's core.

WILLIAM BUTLER YEATS

Stopping by Woods on a Snowy Evening

Whose woods these are I think I know.
His house is in the village though;
He will not see me stopping here
To watch his woods fill up with snow.

My little horse must think it queer
To stop without a farmhouse near
Between the woods and frozen lake
The darkest evening of the year.

He gives his harness bells a shake
To ask if there is some mistake.
The only other sound's the sweep
Of easy wind and downy flake.

The woods are lovely, dark and deep,
But I have promises to keep,
And miles to go before I sleep,
And miles to go before I sleep.

ROBERT FROST

Mouse's Nest

I found a ball of grass among the hay
And progged it as I passed and went away;
And when I looked I fancied something stirred,
And turned agen and hoped to catch the bird –
When out an old mouse bolted in the wheats
With all her young ones hanging at her teats;
She looked so odd and so grotesque to me,
I ran and wondered what the thing could be,
And pushed the knapweed bunches where I stood;
Then the mouse hurried from the craking brood.
The young ones squeaked, and as I went away
She found her nest again among the hay.
The water o'er the pebbles scarce could run
And broad old cesspools glittered in the sun.

JOHN CLARE

Fisherman's Tale

By the canal
I was quietly fishing
when a bowler hat
floated by,
stopped level with my eye
and began to rise.

Below it was a man's head
wearing spectacles;
he asked,
'This way to Brackley?'
'Straight ahead.'
The face sank back
beneath the wet,
but I was thinking
Brackley's seven miles,
it's getting late;
perhaps he doesn't know
how far.

I tapped the hat
with my rod; again
the face rose; 'Yes?'
'You'll need to hurry
to arrive before dark.'
'Don't worry,' he said;
I'm on my bike.'

IRENE RAWNSLEY

Ducks Don't Shop in Sainsbury's

You can't get millet at Sainsbury's
and they don't sell grass or weed
it's a total dead loss
for heather and moss
and they don't stock sunflower seed.

They've got some fish in the freezer
but they're low on rats and mice
and you're out of luck
if you're a debonair duck
and you want to buy something nice

'cos none of their bread is stale
and they've stopped selling hay and straw.
Let's face it, if you were a duck in Sainsbury's,
you'd be heading for the exit door!

GARY BOSWELL

Vailima

Blows the wind today, and the sun and the rain
    are flying,
  Blows the wind on the moors today and now,
Where about the grave of the martyrs the whaups
    are crying,
  My heart remembers how!

Grey recumbent tombs of the dead in desert
    places,
  Standing stones on the vacant wine-red moor,
Hills of sheep, and the howes of the silent vanished
    races,
  And winds, austere and pure:

Be it granted me to behold you again in dying,
  Hills of home! and to hear again the call;
Hear about the graves of the martyrs the peewees
    crying,
  And hear no more at all.

                    ROBERT LOUIS STEVENSON

whaup: Scottish name for a curlew
howe: small valley

My Heart's in the Highlands

My heart's in the Highlands, my heart is not here;
My heart's in the Highlands a-chasing the deer;
Chasing the wild deer, and following the roe,
My heart's in the Highlands, wherever I go.
Farewell to the Highlands, farewell to the North,
The birth-place of valour, the country of worth;
Wherever I wander, wherever I rove,
The hills of the Highlands for ever I love.

Farewell to the mountains, high cover'd with snow;
Farewell to the straths and green valleys below;
Farewell to the forests and wild-hanging woods;
Farewell to the torrents and loud-pouring floods.
My heart's in the Highlands, my heart is not here;
My heart's in the Highlands a-chasing the deer;
Chasing the wild deer, and following the roe,
My heart's in the Highlands, wherever I go.

ROBERT BURNS

roe: a small deer
straths: wide valleys

Moving

The van has gone.
The notice saying SOLD
Is taken down.
The family, weary, strained,
Begins to settle,
Uncomfortable, in the house
Not yet their home.
Tear-stained and lonely
The youngest boy escapes
Into the garden,
Presses his back for comfort
Against the plum tree's
Blackly knobbled bark.

A splutter of dry leaves.
A shiver through the long grass,
And then the hedgehog comes.
Scuttering, uncertain,
Pushing through the daisies
A mere heart's beat away.
It stops, nose twitching,
Scents the evening air –
And rests a moment,
Still, and unafraid.

The boy watches,
Smiles, and feels his pain
Retreat. 'All right,'
He thinks. 'This place will be
All right. Perhaps . . .
I'll LIKE it here.'

JENNIFER CURRY

School Trip

I saw a man in a cardboard box
I saw a lady too,
Her head was wrapped in paper,
She only had one shoe.
We went and saw where Nelson is
We visited St Paul's,
We visited the Palace
and we climbed the city walls.

We saw the Tower Bridge open,
We went and saw Big Ben

   . . . but I remember ladies
   and boxes full of men.

PETER DIXON

Index of First Lines

A centipede was happy quite	25
All along the backwater	12
Blows the wind today, and the sun and the rain are flying	102
Brown and furry	24
By the canal	100
Cat!	10
Clang! Clang! Clang!	72
Clarissa did the washing up	66
Cottonwool clouds loiter	41
Dark brown is the river	96
Dig the ditch and raise the mound	32
Do diddle di do	50
Double, double toil and trouble	27
Get set, ready now, jump right in	91
He was a rat, and she was a rat	17
'I didn't come out of my mummy's tummy	92
I found a ball of grass among the hay	99
I hear leaves drinking rain	42
I love the	86
I saw a donkey	16
I saw a jolly hunter	77
I saw a man in a cardboard box	106
I wanna be the leader	91
I will arise and go now, and go to Innisfree	97
In Hans' old mill his three black cats	19
In the crocus-bed I saw her	37

In the house	76
In the low tide pools	23
Into the kitchen	88
Into the street the Piper stept	18
It so nice to have a Granny	85
last year when Mama died	82
Let's think of eggs	63
Little Willie from his mirror	67
Loveliest of trees, the cherry now	36
Mud is very nice to feel	43
My father he died, but I never knew how	60
My heart's in the Highlands, my heart is not here	103
Nymph, nymph, what are your beads?	28
Oh! There once a swagman camped in a billabong	68
Once, when I wasn't very big	58
Over the hills	26
Run of is Jessy Watson fair	67
Said the Table to the Chair	56
Silently the snow settles on the scaffolding	49
Sing a song of people	64
Snorri Pig had a curly tail	21
Some fathers work at the office, others work at the store	78
Summer is icumen in	39
The Chief Defect of Henry King	62
The earth was green, the sky was blue	38
The friendly cow, all red and white	20
The gingham dog and the calico cat	52
The seeds I sowed	34

The sun went down beyond yon hill, across yon dreary moor	74
The van has gone	104
The Vulture eats between his meals	14
There was a man	70
They're at it again	47
This house has been far out at sea all night	44
Through every nook and every cranny	84
Tom, take the baby out of the fridge	89
Troll sat alone on his eat of stone	30
Twinkle	13
Up on their brooms and Witches stream	29
We don't mention Frank	95
When cats run home and light is come	22
When I'm an aunt I shan't	94
Whenever the moon and stars are set	46
Where the bee sucks, there suck I	33
Where the pools are bright and deep	35
Whose woods these are I think I know	98
'Why can't you tidy your room?' they cry	80
Why this child	83
'Will you walk a little faster?' said a whiting to a snail	54
Winter is icumen in	48
Winter is the king of showmen	49
Yay	90
Yes. I remember Adlestrop	40
You can't get millet at Sainsbury's	101
Your dog? What dog? You mean it? – that!	15

Acknowledgements

The editor and publishers gratefully acknowledge the following for permission to reproduce copyright poems in this book:

'Twinkle Twinkle Firefly' by John Agard from *No Hickory, No Dickory, No Dock*, published by Viking Children's Books, 1991, copyright © John Agard & Grace Nichols, 1991, reprinted by kind permission of John Agard c/o Caroline Sheldon Literary Agency, and 'When Boss Away, Jackass Take Holiday' by John Agard from *Say It Again, Granny*, published by The Bodley Head, reprinted by permission of Random House UK Ltd; 'The Firemen' by James K. Baxter from *The Treehouse*, published by Price Milburn Ltd, New Zealand, reprinted by permission of Mrs J. C. Baxter; 'Henry King' and 'The Vulture' by Hilaire Belloc from *Complete Verse*, published by Pimlico, a division of Random Century, reprinted by permission of the Peters, Fraser & Dunlop Group Ltd; 'The Cat and the Pig' by Gerard Benson from *The Magnificent Callisto*, published by Blackie, 1992, copyright © Gerard Benson, 1992, reprinted by permission of the publisher; 'Ducks Don't Shop in Sainsbury's' by Gary Boswell from *Toughie Toffee* edited by David Orme, published by HarperCollins Publishers Ltd, reprinted by permission of the publisher; 'I Saw a Jolly Hunter' by Charles Causley from *Collected Poems*, published by Macmillan, reprinted by permission of David Higham Associates; 'Suzie's New Dog' by John Ciardi from *Fast And Slow*, copyright © 1975 by John Ciardi, reprinted by permission of Houghton Mifflin Co., all rights reserved; 'Moving' by Jennifer Curry from *Prickly Poems*, published by Hutchinson, 1992, copyright © Jennifer Curry, 1992, reprinted by permission of the author; 'Five Eyes', 'Jim Jay', 'The Ride-By-Nights' and 'Seeds' by Walter de la Mare from *The Complete Poems of Walter de la Mare*, published by Faber & Faber, 1969, reprinted by permission of the Literary Trustees of Walter de la Mare, and The Society of Authors as their representative; 'Beltane Eve' by William Croft Dickinson from *Borrobil*, published by Jonathan Cape, 1944, copyright © The Estate of William Croft Dickinson, 1944, reprinted by permission of the executors; 'School Trip' by Peter Dixon from *Big Billy*, published by Peche Luna, 1992, copyright © Peter Dixon, reprinted by permission of the author; 'Cat' by Eleanor Farjeon from *The Children's Bells*, published by Oxford University Press, reprinted by permission of David Higham Associates; 'Stopping by Woods on a Snowy Evening' by Robert Frost from *The Poetry of Robert Frost* edited by Edward Connery Lathem, published by Jonathan Cape & Holt Reinhardt, published by permission of Random House UK Ltd; 'Crab' by Ted Hughes from *Seven Ages* chosen by David Owen, published by Michael Joseph, 1992, copyright © Ted Hughes, reprinted by permission of the author, and 'My Father' from *Meet My Folks*, and 'Wind' from *The Hawk in the Rain* by Ted Hughes, published by Faber & Faber Ltd, reprinted by permission of the publisher; 'What Jenny Knows' by Jackie Kay from *Two's Company*, published by Blackie, 1992, copyright © Jackie Kay, 1992, reprinted by permission of the publisher; 'The Witches' Ride' by Karla Kuskin from *Dogs & Dragons, Trees & Dreams*, published by HarperCollins Publishers, US, copyright © Karla Kuskin, 1989, reprinted by permission of the publisher; 'Sing a Song of People' by Lois Lenski from *The Life I Live*, reprinted by permission of The Lois Lenski Covey Foundation Inc.; 'When' by Shelagh McGee from *Smile Please*, published by Robson Books Ltd, reprinted by permission of the publisher; 'The Leader' by Roger McGough from *Sky in the Pie*, published by Kestrel, 1983, copyright © Roger McGough, 1983, and 'Storm' by Roger McGough from *After the Merrymaking*, published by Jonathan Cape, both reprinted by permission of the Peters, Fraser & Dunlop Group Ltd; 'Cat and Crocuses' by Eva Martin from *The Poet's Cat* edited by Mona Gooden, published by George G.

Harrap & Co., reprinted by permission of the publisher; 'Teevee' by Eve Merriam from *Catch a Little Rhyme*, copyright © Eve Merriam, 1966, copyright © renewed 1994 Dee Michel & Guy Michel, reprinted by permission of Marian Reiner; 'Granny' by Spike Milligan from *Silly Verse for Kids*, published by Dobson Books, 1959, copyright © Spike Milligan Productions Ltd, 1959, reprinted by permission of Norma Farnes; 'The Fridge' and 'Working in Winter' by John Mole from *Catching the Spider*, published by Blackie Children's Books, 1992, copyright © John Mole, 1992, reprinted by permission of the publisher; 'The Poultries' by Ogden Nash from *Family Reunion*, published by Little, Brown, 1950, copyright © Ogden Nash, 1950, renewed, and 'Winter Morning' by Ogden Nash from *The New Nutcracker and Other Verses*, published by Little, Brown, 1962, copyright © Ogden Nash, 1962, reprinted by permission of Curtis Brown Ltd; 'Granny' by Grace Nichols from *No Hickory, No Dickory, No Dock*, published by Viking Children's Books, 1991, copyright © John Agard and Grace Nichols, 1991, reprinted by permission of the publisher; 'Poor Grandma' by Grace Nichols from *Come On Into My Tropical Garden*, published by A. & C. Black, reproduced with permission of Curtis Brown Group Ltd, London on behalf of Grace Nichols, copyright © Grace Nichols, 1988; 'The Rival Arrives' by Brian Patten from *Thawing Frozen Frogs*, published by Viking Children's Books, 1990, copyright © Brian Patten, 1990, reprinted by permission of Rogers, Coleridge & White Ltd; 'Ancient Music' by Ezra Pound from *Collected Shorter Poems*, published by Faber & Faber Ltd, reprinted by permission of the publisher; 'Fisherman's Tale' by Irene Rawnsley from *Toughie Toffee* edited by David Orme, published by HarperCollins Publishers Ltd, reprinted by permission of the publisher; 'The Skyfoogle' by Michael Rosen from *The Hypnotiser*, published by André Deutsch Children's Books, an imprint of Scholastic Publications Ltd, reprinted by permission of the publisher; 'A Hot Day' by A. S. J. Tessimond, reprinted by kind permission of Hubert Nicholson; 'The Stone Troll' by J. R. R. Tolkien from *The Adventures of Tom Bombadil*, published by HarperCollins Publishers Ltd, reprinted by permission of the publisher; 'Clumsy Clarissa' by Colin West from *Not to be Taken Seriously*, published by Hutchinson, copyright © Colin West, reprinted by permission of the author, and 'Frank' by Colin West from *Toughie Toffee* edited by David Orme, published by HarperCollins Publishers Ltd, reprinted by permission of the publisher.

Every effort has been made to trace copyright holders, but in a few cases this has proved impossible. The editor and publishers apologize for these cases of unwilling copyright transgression and would like to hear from any copyright holders not acknowledged.